THE USBORNE INTERNET-LINKED

FIRST THOUSAND WORDS

IN RUSSIAN

With Internet-linked pronunciation guide

Heather Amery

Illustrated by Stephen Cartwright

Russian edition translated and typeset by AST-Press, Moscow
Edited by Mairi Mackinnon

Russian language consultants: Clare Mitchell and Marina Demidova

Reading the Russian alphabet

Russian is written in the Cyrillic (say *sirilick*) alphabet. This may look strange at first, but it is fairly easy to learn. Once you have looked at the alphabet, try writing your name in the Cyrillic alphabet, and then some other names. This is a good way to learn the letters and their sounds.

There are many Russian words that are very similar to English, but are written in the Cyrillic alphabet and pronounced in the Russian way. For example, a mask is маска, "*maska*", and a lamp is лампа, "*lampa*". You will be surprised by the number of words you recognize.

If you look at the list below, you will see that some Cyrillic letters look like our alphabet, but some look very different. Be careful, because the ones that look the same may have a different sound: В, for example, sounds like *v* in van, Р sounds like *r* in root and Н sounds like *n* in net. So when you see ванна you say "*vanna*" (bath), when you see радио you say "*radeeo*" (radio) and when you see банан you say "*banan*" (banana).

Vowels

printed		written		
А	а	*А*	*а*	a as in *mat*
О	о	*О*	*о*	aw as in *paw*
Э	э	*э*	*э*	e as in *bed*
У	у	*У*	*у*	oo as in *boot*
Ы	ы	*ы*	*ы*	i as in *rip* (tongue pushed back)
Я	я	*Я*	*я*	ya as in *yak*
Ё	ё	*Ё*	*ё*	yaw as in *yawn*
Е	е	*Е*	*е*	ye as in *yet*
Ю	ю	*ю*	*ю*	yoo as in *useful*
И	и	*И*	*и*	ee as in *meet*
Й	й	*Й*	*й*	y as in *boy*

Hard and soft vowels

Hard: а о э у ы
Soft: я ё е ю й

For each English vowel you will notice that there are two in Russian, a hard and a soft. The soft vowel has a "y" sound before it. To hear the difference, practice saying а я, "*a ya*".

Consonants

printed		written		
Б	б	*Б*	*б*	b as in *book*
В	в	*В*	*в*	v as in *van*
Г	г	*Г*	*г*	g as in *get*
Д	д	*D*	*g*	d as in *day*
Ж	ж	*Ж*	*ж*	zh like the s in *pleasure*
З	з	*З*	*з*	z as in *zoo*
К	к	*К*	*к*	k as in *kit*
Л	л	*Л*	*л*	l as in *table*, before a hard vowel, or l as in *leaf*, before a soft vowel
М	м	*М*	*м*	m as in *milk*
Н	н	*Н*	*н*	n as in *net*
П	п	*П*	*п*	p as in *pot*
Р	р	*Р*	*р*	r as in *rock*
С	с	*С*	*с*	s as in *sit*
Т	т	*Т*	*m̄*	t as in *top*
Ф	ф	*Ф*	*ф*	f as in *fan*
Х	х	*Х*	*х*	ch as in Scottish *loch*
Ц	ц	*Ц*	*ц*	ts as in *cats*
Ч	ч	*Ч*	*ч*	ch as in *cheese*
Ш	ш	*Ш*	*ш*	sh as in *fresh*
Щ	щ	*Щ*	*щ*	shch as in *fresh cheese*
Ъ	ъ	*Ъ*	*ъ*	'hard sign' (very rare), gives the letter before it a 'hard' sound.
Ь	ь	*Ь*	*ь*	'soft sign', gives the letter before it a 'soft' sound.

On every big picture across two pages, there is a little yellow duck to look for. Can you find it?

Saying Russian words

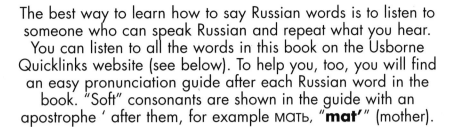

The best way to learn how to say Russian words is to listen to someone who can speak Russian and repeat what you hear. You can listen to all the words in this book on the Usborne Quicklinks website (see below). To help you, too, you will find an easy pronunciation guide after each Russian word in the book. "Soft" consonants are shown in the guide with an apostrophe ' after them, for example мать, "**mat'**" (mother).

In English, many words have a part that is stressed, or sounds stronger. For example, in "window" you stress "win". It is the same in Russian, and in this book you will see that the part you stress has been shown **like this**. So when you read дельфин, say "dyel'**feen**" (dolphin), stressing "**feen**".

When you see the letter о you need to notice whether it is stressed or not. If it is stressed, say "aw" as in "paw", but if it is not stressed, say "a" as in "mat". For example, when you read футбол, say "foot**bol**" (football), but when you read шоколад, say "shaka**lad**" (chocolate).

Hear the words on the Internet

You can listen to all the words in this book, read by a native Russian speaker, on the Usborne Quicklinks Website. Just go to **www.usborne-quicklinks.com** and enter the keywords **1000 russian**. There you can:

- listen to the first thousand words in Russian
- find links to other useful websites about Russia and the Russian language.

Your computer needs a sound card (almost all computers have these) and may also need a small program, called an audio player, such as RealPlayer® or Windows® Media Player. These programs are free, and if you don't already have a copy, you can download one from the Usborne Quicklinks Website.

Note for parents and guardians

Please ensure that your children read and follow the Internet safety guidelines displayed on the Usborne Quicklinks Website.

The links in Usborne Quicklinks are regularly reviewed and updated. However, the content of a website may change at any time, and Usborne Publishing is not responsible for the content on any website other than its own. We recommend that children are supervised while on the Internet, that they do not use Internet chat rooms and that you use Internet filtering software to block unsuitable material. For more information, see the **Net Help** area on the Usborne Quicklinks Website.

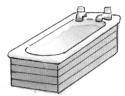

ванна
vanna

мыло
mila

кран
kran

туалетная бумага
tooa**lyet**-naya boo**ma**ga

зубная щётка
zoo**bna**ya **shchot**ka

вода
va**da**

унитаз
oonee**taz**

губка
goobka

раковина
rakaveena

душ
doosh

полотенце
pala**tyen**tse

Дома
doma

ванная
vannaya

гостиная
ga**stee**naya

кровать
kra**vat'**

зубная паста
zoo**bna**ya **pas**ta

радио
radeeo

подушка
pa**doosh**ka

компакт-диск
kam**pakt deesk**

ковёр
ka**vyor**

софа
sa**fa**

СТУЛ
stool

пуховое одеяло
poo**ho**vaye adye**ya**la

расчёска
ras**chos**ka

простыня
prasti**nya**

коврик
kovreek

ШКАФ
shkaf

ПОДУШКА
pa**doosh**ka

СПАЛЬНЯ
spal'nya

КОМОД
ka**mod**

зеркало
zyerkala

щётка
shchotka

ЛАМПА
lampa

ХОЛЛ
holl

КАРТИНЫ
kar**tee**ni

ВЕШАЛКА
vyeshalka

ТЕЛЕФОН
tele**fon**

батарея
bata**ryey**a

видеокассета
veedeokas**syet**a

газета
ga**zyet**a

СТОЛ
stol

письма
pees'ma

ЛЕСТНИЦА
lestneetsa

Кухня

koohnya

ХОЛОДИЛЬНИК
haladeel'neek

СТАКАНЫ
stakani

ЧАСЫ
chasi

ТАБУРЕТ
tabooryet

ЧАЙНЫЕ ЛОЖКИ
chayniye lozhkee

ВЫКЛЮЧАТЕЛЬ
viklyoo-chatyel'

СТИРАЛЬНЫЙ ПОРОШОК
steeral'niy parashok

КЛЮЧ
klyooch

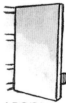

ДВЕРЬ
dver'

МОЙКА
moyka

ПЫЛЕСОС
pilyesos

КАСТРЮЛИ
kastryoolee

ВИЛКИ
veelkee

ФАРТУК
fartook

ГЛАДИЛЬНАЯ ДОСКА
gladeel'naya daska

МУСОР
moosar

6

чайник
chayneek

ножи
na**zhee**

швабра
shvabra

ТРЯПКА
ДЛЯ ПЫЛИ
tryapka dlya **pi**lee

кафель
kafyel'

ЩЁТКА
shchotka

СТИРАЛЬНАЯ
МАШИНА
stee**ral'**naya ma**shee**na

СОВОК
sa**vok**

ЯЩИК
yashcheek

БЛЮДЦА
blyootsa

СКОВОРОДА
skavara**da**

ПЛИТА
plee**ta**

ЛОЖКИ
lozhkee

ТАРЕЛКИ
ta**ryel**kee

УТЮГ
oo**tyoog**

КЛАДОВКА
kla**dov**ka

кухонное
полотенце
koohannaye pala**tyen**tse

чашки
chashkee

спички
speechkee

ЩЁТКА
shchotka

миски
meeskee

тачка
tachka

улей
ooley

улитка
oo**leet**ka

кирпичи
keerpee**chee**

голубь
goloob'

лопата
la**pa**ta

божья коровка
bozh'ya ka**rov**ka

мусорный бак
moosarniy **bak**

семена
syeme**na**

сарай
sa**ray**

Сад sad

лейка
leyka

червяк
cher**vyak**

цветы
tsvye**ti**

поливальная установка
palee-**val**'naya oosta**nov**ka

мотыга
ma**ti**ga

оса
a**sa**

ПЧЕЛА
pchye**la**

СОВОК
sa**vok**

КОСТЬ
kost'

ЖИВАЯ ИЗГОРОДЬ
zhi**va**ya **eez**garad'

ВИЛЫ
veeli

ГАЗОНОКОСИЛКА
gazona-ka**seel**ka

ТРОПИНКА
tra**peen**ka

ЛИСТЬЯ
leest'ya

ДЕРЕВО
deryeva

ДЫМ
dim

ГУСЕНИЦА
goosyeneetsa

ГРАБЛИ
grablee

ГНЕЗДО
gnyez**do**

ВЕТКИ
vyetkee

ТЕПЛИЦА
tye**pleet**sa

ТРАВА
tra**va**

КОЛЯСКА
ka**lyas**ka

ЛЕСТНИЦА
lestneetsa

КОСТЁР
ka**styor**

ШЛАНГ
shlang

9

тиски
teeskee

наждачная бумага
nazh**dach**naya
boo**ma**ga

дрель
dryel'

лестница
lestneetsa

пила
pee**la**

опилки
a**peel**kee

календарь
kalyen**dar'**

Мастерская
mastyer**ska**ya

шурупы
shoo**roo**pi

ящик для инструментов
yashcheek dlya eenstroo-**myen**tav

отвёртка
at**vyort**ka

доска
da**ska**

стружки
strooshkee

перочинный нож
pyera**cheen**niy **nozh**

10

КНОПКИ
knopkee

ПАУК
pa-**ook**

ВИНТЫ
veen**ti**

ГАЙКИ
gaykee

ПАУТИНА
pa-oo**tee**na

бочка
bochka

муха
mooha

топор
ta**por**

рулетка
roo**lyet**ka

МОЛОТОК
mala**tok**

НАПИЛЬНИК
na**peel'**neek

банка с
краской
banka
s**kras**koy

дрова
dra**va**

ГВОЗДИ
gvozdee

ВЕРСТАК
vyer**stak**

банки
bankee

рубанок
roo**ba**nak

11

Улица

oоleetsa

магазин
magazeen

яма
yama

кафе
ka-fe

скорая помощь
skoraya pomashch'

тротуар
tratooar

антенна
antenna

труба
trooba

крыша
krisha

экскаватор
ekskavatar

гостиница
gasteeneetsa

автобус
avtoboos

мужчина
moozhcheena

милицейская машина
meelee-tseyskaya masheena

трубы
troobi

отбойный
молоток
atboyniy malatok

школа
shkola

площадка для иг
plashchadka dlya eegr

12

такси
tak**see**

переход
pere**hod**

фабрика
fabreeka

грузовик
grooza**veek**

светофор
svyeta**for**

кинотеатр
keenate**atr**

фургон
foor**gon**

каток
ka**tok**

прицеп
pree**tsep**

дом
dom

рынок
rinak

лестница
lestneetsa

мотоцикл
mata**tseek**l

дом
dom

велосипед
velasee**pyed**

пожарная машина
pa**zhar**naya ma**shee**na

милиционер
meelee-tseea**nyer**

машина
ma**shee**na

женщина
zhenshcheena

**уличный
фонарь**
ooleechniy
fa**nar'**

13

Магазин игрушек

magazeen
eegrooshek

железная дорога
zhelyeznaya daroga

игральные кости
eegral'niye kostee

блок-флейта
blok-fleyta

робот
robat

барабаны
barabani

ожерелье
azheryel'ye

фотоаппарат
fota-apparat

бусы
boosi

куклы
kookli

гитара
geetara

кольцо
kal'tso

кукольный дом
kookal'niy dom

губная гармошка
goobnaya garmoshka

свисток
sveestok

кубики
koobeekee

замок
zamak

подводная лодка
padvodnaya lodka

труба
trooba

стрелы
stryeli

14

лук
look

парашют
para**shoot**

яхта
yahta

грим
greem

каток
ka**tok**

маски
maskee

гоночная машина
gonachnaya ma**shee**na

лошадь-качалка
loshad'-ka**chal**ka

копилка
ka**peel**ka

шарики
shareekee

марионетки
mareea-**nyet**kee

рояль
ra**yal'**

космонавты
kasma**naf**ti

ракета
ra**kye**ta

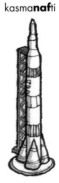

подъёмный кран
pa**dyom**niy **kran**

пластилин
plastee**leen**

ружьё
roozh'**yo**

солдатики
sal**da**teekee

краски
kraskee

15

качели
ka**chyel**ee

песочница
pe**soch**neetsa

ПИКНИК
peek**neek**

ВОЗДУШНЫЙ
змей
vaz**doosh**niy
z**myey**

мороженое
ma**ro**zhenaye

собака
sa**ba**ka

КАЛИТКА
ka**leet**ka

тропинка
tra**peen**ka

лягушка
lya**goosh**ka

горка для катания
gorka dlya ka**ta**neeya

Парк

park

скамейка
ska**myey**ka

головастики
gala**vas**teekee

озеро
ozyera

РОЛИКИ
roleekee

куст
koost

малыш
ma**lish**

скейтборд
skeytbord

земля
zyem**lya**

прогулочная коляска
pra**goo**-lachnaya ka**lyas**ka

качели
ka**chyel**ee

дети
dyetee

трёхколёсный велосипед
tryohkal-**yos**niy
vyela-see**pyed**

ПТИЦЫ
pteetsi

забор
za**bor**

МЯЧ
myach

ЯХТА
yahta

бечёвка
bye**chov**ka

ЛУЖА
loozha

УТЯТА
ooty**ta**

скакалка
ska**kal**ka

клумба
kloomba

лебеди
lyebedee

поводок
pava**dok**

УТКИ
ootkee

деревья
dye**ryev'**ya

Зоопарк

zaapark

панда
panda

крыло
kri**lo**

орёл
ar**yol**

бегемот
bege**mot**

летучая мышь
lye**too**chaya **mish'**

горилла
ga**reel**la

лапы
lapi

кенгуру
kengoo**roo**

обезьяна
abyez'**ya**na

айсберг
aysbyerg

пингвин
peen**gveen**

ХВОСТ
hvost

ВОЛК
volk

перья
pyer'ya

крокодил
kraka**deel**

медведь
myed**vyed'**

пеликан
pelee**kan**

страус
straoos

дельфин
dyel'**feen**

ЛЕВ
lyev

ЛЬВЯТА
l'**vya**ta

жираф
zhi**raf**

18

рога
ra**ga**

олень
a**len'**

вербглюд
vyer**blyood**

тюлень
tyoo**len'**

белый медведь
byeliy myed**vyed'**

черепаха
chere**pa**ha

хобот
hobat

слон
slon

носорог
nasa**rog**

бизон
bee**zon**

бобр
bobr

коза
ka**za**

зебра
zyebra

змея
zme**ya**

акула
a**koo**la

кит
keet

тигр
teegr

леопард
lyea**pard**

19

железная дорога
zhe**lyez**naya da**ro**ga

локомотив
lakama**teev**

буфера
boofye**ra**

вагоны
va**go**ni

машинист
mashee**neest**

товарный поезд
ta**var**niy **po**yest

платформа
plat**for**ma

контролёр
kantra**lyor**

чемодан
chema**dan**

касса-автомат
kassa-avta**mat**

Путешествие
pootye-**shest**veeye

вертолёт
vyerta**lyot**

Вокзал vak**zal**

Гараж ga**razh**

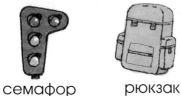

семафор
sema**for**

рюкзак
ryook**zak**

фары
fari

двигатель
dveegatyel'

колесо
kalye**so**

аккумулятор
akoomoo-**lya**tar

Аэропорт

a-era**port**

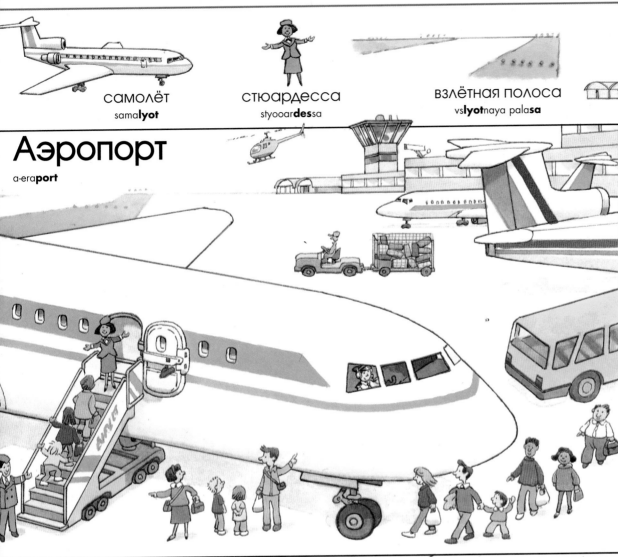

самолёт
sama**lyot**

стюардесса
styooar**des**sa

взлётная полоса
vs**lyot**naya pala**sa**

стюард
styoo**ard**

пилот
pee**lot**

автомойка
afta**moy**ka

багажник
ba**gazh**neek

бензин
byen**zeen**

аварийная машина
ava**ree**naya ma**shee**na

бензоколонка
byenzaka**lon**ka

АВТОМОЙКА

бензовоз
byenza**voz**

гаечный ключ
gayechniy **klyooch**

шина
sheena

капот
ka**pot**

масло
masla

21

ветряная мельница
vyetrya-**na**ya **myel'**neetsa

воздушный шар
vaz**doosh**niy **shar**

бабочка
babachka

ящерица
yashchereetsa

камни
kamnee

лиса
lee**sa**

ручей
roo**chey**

дорожный указатель
da**rozh**niy oo**ka**za**tyel'**

шлюз
shlyooz

Сельская местность

syel'skaya
myestnast'

гора
ga**ra**

белка
byelka

лес
lyes

барсук
bar**sook**

река
rye**ka**

дорога
da**ro**ga

палатки
palatkee

канал
kanal

брёвна
bryovna

деревня
deryevnya

МОТЫЛЁК
matilyok

МОСТ
most

баржа
barzha

ВОДОПАД
vadapad

СОВА
sava

туннель
toonel'

ЛИСЯТА
leesyata

крот
krot

рыбак
ribak

КАМНИ
kamnee

жаба
zhaba

поезд
poyest

автофургон
aftafoorgon

ХОЛМ
holm

23

стог
stok

колли
kollee

утки
ootkee

ягнята
yag**nya**ta

пруд
prood

цыплята
tsi**plya**ta

чердак
cher**dak**

свинарник
svee**nar**neek

бык
bik

утята
ooty**a**ta

курятник
koo**ryat**neek

трактор
traktar

Ферма **fyer**ma

петух
pye**tooh**

гуси
goosee

цистерна
tsees**ter**na

амбар
am**bar**

земля
zyem**lya**

тележка
tye**lyesh**ka

24

фермер
fyermyer

поле
polye

куры
koori

телёнок
tye**lyo**nak

забор
za**bor**

седло
syed**lo**

коровник
ka**rov**neek

корова
ka**ro**va

плуг
ploog

сад
sad

конюшня
ka**nyoosh**nya

поросята
para**sya**ta

пастушка
pa**stoosh**ka

индюки
eendyoo**kee**

пугало
poogala

дом на ферме
dom na **fyer**mye

сено
syena

овцы
ovtsi

брикеты соломы
bree**kyet**i sa**lo**mi

лошадь
loshad'

свиньи
sveen'ee

25

парусник
paroosneek

раковина
rakaveena

У моря
oo **mo**rya

море
morye

весло
vyes**lo**

маяк
ma**yak**

лопата
la**pa**ta

ведро
vye**dro**

морская звезда
mar**ska**ya zvyez**da**

замок из песка
zamak eez pyes**ka**

зонтик
zonteek

флаг
flag

моряк
ma**ryak**

краб
krab

чайка
chayka

остров
ostrav

моторка
ma**tor**ka

водный лыжник
vodniy **lizh**neek

ВОЛНЫ
volni

ШЛЯПА
shlyapa

УТЁС
ootyos

КОРАБЛЬ
karabl'

БАЙДАРКА
baydarka

КАНАТ
kanat

ГАЛЬКА
gal'ka

ВОДОРОСЛИ
vodaraslee

СЕТЬ
syet'

ВЕСЛО
vyeslo

РЫБАЧЬЯ ЛОДКА
ribach'ya lodka

ЛАСТЫ
lasti

ОСЛИК
osleek

РЫБА
riba

КУПАЛЬНИК
koopal'neek

ТАНКЕР
tankyer

ПЛЯЖ
plyazh

ВЁСЕЛЬНАЯ ЛОДКА
vyosel'naya lodka

ШЕЗЛОНГ
shezlong

27

НОЖНИЦЫ
nozhneetsi

2 + 2 = 4
3 + 2 = 5

примеры
pree**myer**i

резинка
rye**zeen**ka

линейка
lee**nyey**ka

фотографии
fata**gra**fee

фломастеры
fla**mas**teri

КНОПКИ
knopkee

краски
kraskee

мальчик
mal'cheek

карандаш
karan**dash**

В ШКОЛЕ
v**shkol**ye

ДОСКА
da**ska**

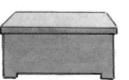

ПИСЬМЕННЫЙ СТОЛ
pees'myenniy **stol**

КНИГИ
kneegee

ручка
roochka

КЛЕЙ
kley

мел
myel

рисунок
ree**soo**nak

28

мусорное ведро
moosarnaye vye**dro**

учительница
oo**chee**tel'neetsa

коробка
ka**rop**ka

карта
karta

кисточка
keestochka

потолок
pata**lok**

стена
stye**na**

ПОЛ
pol

тетрадь
tyet**rad'**

абвгдеёжз
ийклмнопр
стуфхцчш
щъыьэюя

алфавит
alfa**veet**

значок
zna**chok**

аквариум
ak**va**reeooom

бумага
boo**ma**ga

жалюзи
zhalyoozee

…рная ручка
…yer**na**ya **rooch**ka

растение
ra**styen**eeye

глобус
globoos

девочка
dyevachka

карандаши
karanda**shee**

настольная
лампа
na**stol**'naya **lam**pa

мольберт
mal'**byert**

29

Больница

bal'**neet**sa

медбрат
myed**brat**

вата
vata

лекарство
lye**kar**stva

лифт
leeft

халат
ha**lat**

костыли
kasti**lee**

таблетки
ta**blyet**kee

поднос
pad**nos**

часы
cha**si**

термометр
tyer**mo**metr

занавеска
zana-**vyes**ka

плюшевый мишка
plyoosheviy **meesh**ka

яблоко
yablaka

гипс
geeps

бинт
beent

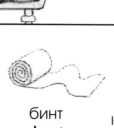

кресло-каталка
kryesla-ka**tal**ka

картинка-
конструктор
kar**teen**ka-kan**strook**tar

врач
vrach

шприц
sh**preets**

Врач
vrach

ШЛЁПАНЦЫ
shlyopantsi

КОМПЬЮТЕР
kamp'**yoo**ter

ПЛАСТЫРЬ
plastir'

БАНАН
ba**nan**

ВИНОГРАД
veena**grad**

КОРЗИНА
kar**zee**na

ИГРУШКИ
ee**groosh**kee

ГРУША
groosha

ОТКРЫТКИ
at**krit**kee

ПОДГУЗНИК
pad**goos**neek

ПАЛКА
palka

ТЕЛЕВИЗОР
tele**vee**zar

НОЧНАЯ РУБАШКА
nach**na**ya roo**bash**ka

ПИЖАМА
pee**zha**ma

АПЕЛЬСИН
apel'**seen**

САЛФЕТКИ
sal**fyet**kee

КОМИКСЫ
komeeksi

ПРИЁМНАЯ
pree**yom**naya

31

Вечеринка

vyche**reen**ka

подарки
pa**dar**kee

воздушный шарик
vaz**doosh**niy **sha**reek

шоколад
shaka**lad**

конфета
kan**fyet**a

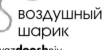

окно
ak**no**

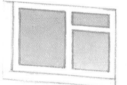

фейерверк
feyer**vyerk**

лента
lyenta

торт
tort

соломинка
sa**lo**meenka

свеча
svye**cha**

гирлянда
geer**lyan**da

игрушки
ee**groosh**kee

мандарин
manda**reen**

САЛЯМИ
sa**lya**mee

кассета
kas**syet**a

сосиска
sa**sees**ka

ЧИПСЫ
cheepsi

МАСКАРАДНЫЕ
КОСТЮМЫ
maska-**rad**niye
kas**tyoo**mi

ВИШНЯ
veeshnya

фруктовый сок
frook**to**viy **sok**

МАЛИНА
ma**lee**na

клубника
kloob**nee**ka

ЛАМПОЧКА
lampachka

бутерброд
bootyer**brod**

масло
masla

печенье
pye**chen'**ye

сыр
seer

хлеб
hlyeb

скатерть
skatyert'

33

Магазин

magazeen

грейпфрут

greypfroot

морковь

markov'

цветная капуста

tsvyetnaya kapoosta

лук-порей

look-parey

гриб

greeb

огурец

agooryets

лимон

leemon

сельдерей

syel'derey

абрикос

abreekos

дыня

dinya

пакет

pakyet

сыр

овощи и фрукты

лук
look

капуста

kapoosta

персик

pyerseek

салат

salat

горох

garoh

помидор

pameedor

яйца
yaytsa

слива
sleeva

мука
moo**ka**

весы
vye**si**

банки
bankee

мясо
myasa

ананас
ana**nas**

йогурт
yogoort

корзина
kar**zee**na

бутылки
boo**til**kee

сумочка
soomachka

кошелёк
kashe**lyok**

деньги
dyen'gee

консервы
kan**syer**vi

тележка
tye**lyesh**ka

картофель
kar**to**fel'

шпинат
shpee**nat**

бобы
ba**bi**

касса
kassa

тыква
tikva

35

Еда ye**da**

завтрак
zavtrak

обед
a**byed**

варёное яйцо
va**ryon**aye yay**tso**

тосты
tosti

джем
djem

кофе
kofye

яичница
ya**eech**neetsa

СЛИВКИ
sleevkee

МОЛОКО
mala**ko**

ХЛОПЬЯ
hlop'ya

какао
ka**ka**o

сахар
sahar

мёд
myod

СОЛЬ
sol'

перец
pyeryets

чай
chay

ЧАЙНИК
chayneek

блины
blee**ni**

булочки
boolachkee

36

ужин
oozheen

ветчина
vyetchee**na**

суп
soop

омлет
am**lyet**

палочки
palachkee

салат
sa**lat**

гамбургер
gamboorgyer

цыплёнок
tsi**plyo**nak

рис
rees

соус
so-oos

спагетти
spa**get**tee

картофельное пюре
kar**to**fel'naye pyoo**re**

пицца
peetsa

чипсы
cheepsi

пудинг
poodeeng

Я ya

ГОЛОВА
gala**va**

ВОЛОСЫ
volasi

ЛИЦО
lee**tso**

рука
roo**ka**

ЛОКОТЬ
lokat'

ЖИВОТ
zhi**vot**

ПАЛЬЦЫ НОГИ
pal'tsi na**gee**

СТУПНЯ
stoop**nya**

НОГА
na**ga**

КОЛЕНО
ka**lyen**a

бровь
brov'

глаз
glaz

нос
nos

щека
shche**ka**

рот
rot

губы
goobi

зубы
zoobi

язык
ya**zik**

подбородок
padba**ro**dak

уши
ooshee

шея
sheya

плечи
plyechee

грудь
grood'

спина
spee**na**

ЯГОДИЦЫ
yaga**deet**si

кисть руки
keest' roo**kee**

большой палец
bal'**shoy pa**lyets

пальцы
pal'tsi

38

Моя одежда

носки
naskee

трусы
troosee

майка
mayka

брюки
bryookee

джинсы
djeensi

футболка
footbolka

юбка
yoopka

рубашка
roobashka

галстук
galstook

шорты
shorti

колготки
kalgotkee

платье
plat'ye

джемпер
djempyer

свитер
sveeter

кофта
kofta

шарф
sharf

носовой платок
nasavoy platok

кроссовки
krassovkee

ботинки
bateenkee

сандалии
sandalee

сапоги
sapagee

перчатки
pyerchatkee

ремень
ryemen'

пряжка
pryashka

молния
molneeya

шнурок
shnoorok

пуговицы
poogaveetsi

петли
pyetlee

карманы
karmani

пальто
pal'to

куртка
koortka

кепка
kyepka

шляпа
shlyapa

39

Люди

lyoodee

повар
povar

танцоры
tan**tsor**i

актёр
ak**tyor**

актриса
ak**tree**sa

певцы
pyev**tsi**

космонавт
kazma**naft**

МЯСНИК
myas**neek**

милиционер
meelee-tseea**nyer**

женщина-
милиционер
zhenshcheena-
meelee-tseea**nyer**

ПЛОТНИК
plotneek

пожарник
pa**zhar**neek

ХУДОЖНИК
hoo**dozh**neek

СУДЬЯ
sood'**ya**

механики
mye**ha**neekee

парикмахер
pareek-**ma**hyer

водитель грузовика
va**dee**tyel' groozavee**ka**

водитель автобуса
va**dee**tyel' av**to**boosa

зубной врач
zoob**noy vrach**

ВОДОЛАЗ
vada**laz**

официант
afee-tsee**ant**

официантка
afee-tsee**ant**ka

почтальон
pachtal'**on**

маляр
ma**lyar**

пекарь
pyekar'

Семья

syem'**ya**

сын
sin

брат
brat

дочь
doch'

сестра
syes**tra**

мать
mat'

жена
zhe**na**

отец
a**tyets**

муж
moozh

тётя
tyotya

дядя
dyadya

двоюродный брат
dva**yoo**radniy **brat**

дедушка
dyedooshka

бабушка
babooshka

41

Занятия
zanyateeya

улыбаться
oolibat'sa

плакать
plakat'

думать
doomat'

слушать
slooshat'

смеяться
smeyat'sa

ловить
laveet'

бросать
brasat'

ломать
lamat'

рисовать
reesavat'

писать
peesat'

рубить
roobeet'

резать
ryezat'

есть
yest'

разговаривать
razga-vareevat'

копать
kapat'

нести
nyestee

пить
peet'

делать
dyelat'

прыгать
prigat'

танцевать
tantsevat'

мыть
mit'

вязать
vyazat'

ползти
palstee

42

играть
eegrat'

смотреть
smatryet'

залезать
zalyezat'

брать
brat'

прыгать
prigat'

драться
drat'sa

спать
spat'

шить
sheet'

ждать
zhdat'

готовить еду
gatoveet' yedoo

прятаться
pryatat'sa

читать
cheetat'

покупать
pakoopat'

толкать
talkat'

петь
pyet'

дуть
doot'

тянуть
tyanoot'

подметать
padmyetat'

собирать
sabeerat'

падать
padat'

идти
eedtee

бежать
byezhat'

сидеть
seedyet'

43

Антонимы

antoneemi

хороший
haroshee

плохой
plahoy

верхний
vyerhnee

нижний
neezhnee

далеко
dalyeko

близко
bleezka

холодный
halodniy

горячий
garyachee

мокрый
mokriy

сухой
soohoy

грязный
gryazniy

чистый
cheestiy

над
nad

под
pod

толстый
tolstiy

тонкий
tonkee

открытый
atkritiy

закрытый
zakritiy

маленький
malyen'kee

большой
bal'shoy

мало
mala

много
mnoga

первый
pyerviy

последний
paslyednee

левый
lyeviy

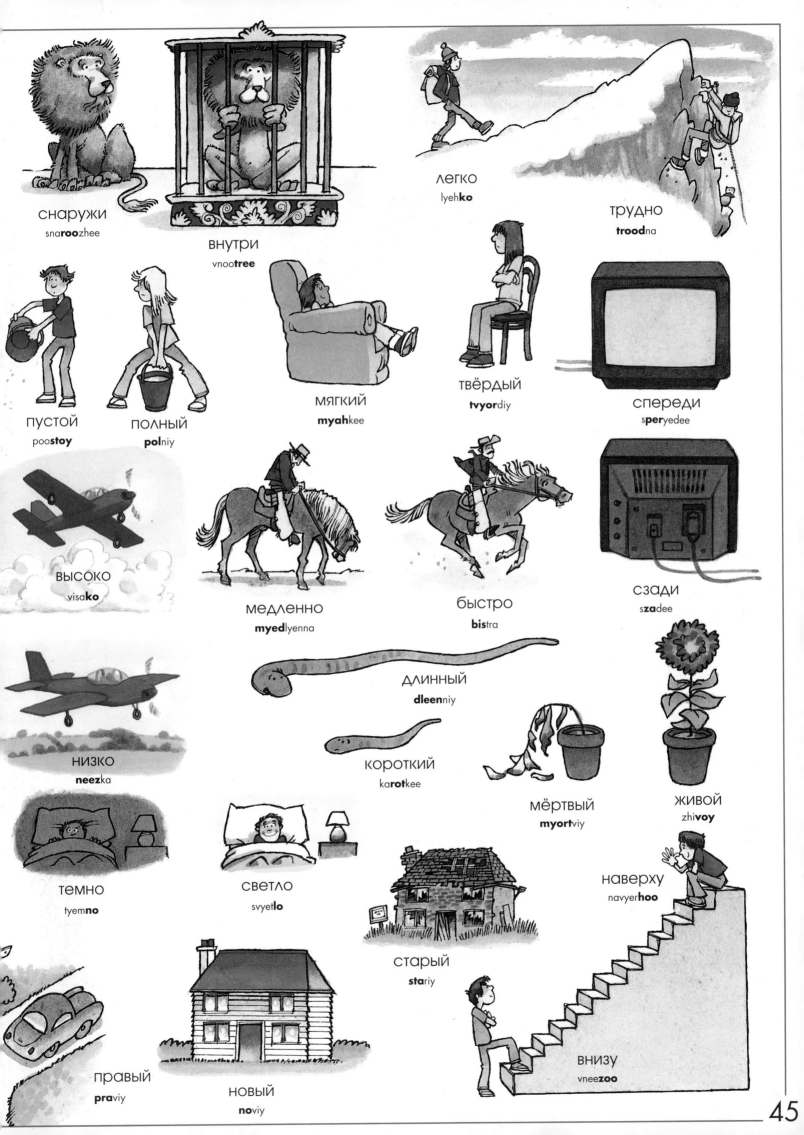

снаружи
snaroozhee

внутри
vnootree

легко
lyehko

трудно
troodna

пустой
poostoy

полный
polniy

мягкий
myahkee

твёрдый
tvyordiy

спереди
speryedee

высоко
visako

медленно
myedlyenna

быстро
bistra

сзади
szadee

низко
neezka

длинный
dleenniy

короткий
karotkee

мёртвый
myortviy

живой
zhivoy

темно
tyemno

светло
svyetlo

старый
stariy

наверху
navyerhoo

правый
praviy

новый
noviy

внизу
vneezoo

45

ДНИ  dnee

понедельник
panye**dyel'**neek

вторник
v**tor**neek

среда
srye**da**

четверг
chet**vyerg**

пятница
pyatneetsa

суббота
soob**bo**ta

воскресенье
vaskre-**syen'**ye

календарь
kalyen**dar'**

утро
ootra

вечер
vyecher

солнце
solntse

ночь
noch'

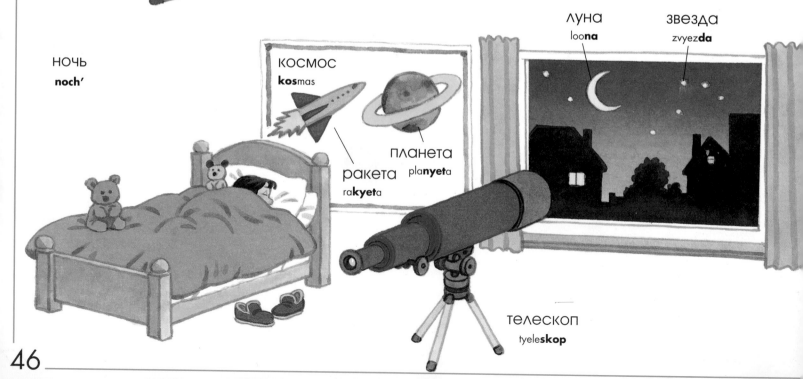

космос
kosmas

ракета
ra**kyet**a

планета
pla**nyet**a

луна
loo**na**

звезда
zvyez**da**

телескоп
tyele**skop**

46

Праздники

prazneekee

день рождения
dyen'
razh**dyen**eeya

свеча
svye**cha**

поздравительная открытка
pazdra-**vee**tel'naya
at**krit**ka

отпуск
otpoosk

подарок
pa**da**rak

праздничный торт
prazneechniy **tort**

свадьба
svad'ba

фотоаппарат
fota-appa**rat**

подружка невесты
pa**droosh**ka nye**vyes**ti

невеста и жених
nye**vyes**ta ee zhe**neeh**

фотограф
fa**to**graf

Рождество
razhdest**vo**

северный олень
syeverniy
a**len'**

Дед Мороз
dyed ma**roz**

сани
sanee

ёлка
yolka

47

Погода
pa**go**da

ЗОНТИК
zonteek

ДОЖДЬ
doshd'

МОЛНИЯ
molneeya

ветер
vyetyer

ТУМАН
too**man**

ТУМАН
too**man**

СНЕГ
snyeg

мороз
ma**roz**

СОЛНЦЕ
solntse

облака
oblaka

небо
nyeba

роса
ra**sa**

радуга
radooga

Времена года
vremye**na go**da

весна
vyes**na**

лето
lyeta

осень
osyen'

зима
zee**ma**

48

Домашние животные

damashneeye
zhivotniye

хомяк
hamyak

ветврач
vyetvrach

будка
bootka

морская свинка
marskaya sveenka

щенок
shchenok

собака
sabaka

корм
korm

волнистый попугайчик
valneestiy papoo-gaycheek

попугай
papoogay

клюв
klyoof

кролик
kroleek

канарейка
kanaryeyka

клетка
klyetka

кошка
koshka

корзина
karzeena

мышь
mish'

котёнок
katyonak

молоко
malako

золотая рыбка
zalataya ribka

Спорт и физкультура

sport ee
feeskool'-**too**ra

баскетбол
baskyet**bol**

гребля
gryeblya

парусный спорт
paroosniy **sport**

виндсёрфинг
veend**syor**feeng

сноубординг
sno-oo**bor**deeng

крикет
kreekyet

каратэ
kara**te**

бита
beeta

ракетка
ra**kyet**ka

теннис
tennees

американский
футбол
amree**kan**skee
foot**bol**

гимнастика
geem**nas**teeka

мяч
m**yach**

удочка
oodachka

наживка
na**zhiv**ka

рыбалка
ri**bal**ka

танцы
tantsi

бейсбол
beys**bol**

прыжки в воду
prish**kee vvo**doo

регби
regbee

бассейн
bas**seyn**

плавание
plavaneeye

бег
byeg

50

стрельба
из лука
stryel'**ba**
eez **loo**ka

мишень
mee**shyen'**

дельтапланеризм
dyel'ta-planye**reezm**

шлем
shlyem

бег трусцой
byeg troos**tsoy**

велоспорт
vyela**sport**

альпинизм
al'pee**neezm**

дзюдо
dzyoo**do**

шкафчик
shkafcheek

лошадь
loshad'

пони
ponee

футбол
foot**bol**

верховая езда
vyerha**va**ya yez**da**

раздевалка
razdye-**val**ka

бадминтон
badmeen**ton**

настольный тенис
na**stol'**niy **ten**nees

коньки
kan'**kee**

фигурное катание
fee**goor**naye ka**ta**neeye

лыжная
палка
lizhnaya **pal**ka

подъёмник
pa**dyom**neek

лыжи
lizhee

горные
лыжи
gorniye **li**zhee

борьба сумо
bar'**ba soo**mo

51

Цвета tsvyeta

оранжевый
a**ran**jeviy

зелёный
zye**lyo**niy

чёрный
chorniy

серый
syeriy

красный
krasniy

коричневый
ka**reech**nyeviy

розовый
rozaviy

белый
byeliy

синий
seenee

пурпурный
poor**poor**niy

жёлтый
zholtiy

Фигуры feegoori

прямоугольник
pryama-oo**gol'**neek

круг
kroog

ромб
romb

конус
konoos

звезда
zvyez**da**

куб
koob

овал
a**val**

треугольник
trye-oo**gol'**neek

квадрат
kva**drat**

полумесяц
paloo-**myes**yats

Числа

cheesla

1	ОДИН a**deen**
2	ДВА **dva**
3	ТРИ **tree**
4	четыре che**tir**ye
5	ПЯТЬ **pyat'**
6	шесть **shest'**
7	семь **syem'**
8	ВОСЕМЬ **vos**yem'
9	девять **dyev**yat'
10	десять **dyes**yat'
11	одиннадцать a**deen**natsat'
12	двенадцать dvye**nat**sat'
13	тринадцать tree**nat**sat'
14	четырнадцать che**tir**-natsat'
15	пятнадцать pyat**nat**sat'
16	шестнадцать shest**nat**sat'
17	семнадцать syem**nat**sat'
18	восемнадцать vasyem-**nat**sat'
19	девятнадцать dyevyat**nat**sat'
20	двадцать **dva**tsat'

53

Луна-парк

loona-**park**

колесо обозрения

kalye**so** aba-**zryen**eeya

карусель

karoo**syel'**

мат

mat

американские горки

ameree-**kan**skeeye **gor**kee

поезд с привидениями

poyest spreevee-**dyen**eeyamee

попкорн

pap**korn**

набрось-кольцо

na**bros'**-kal'**tso**

американские горки

ameree-**kan**skeeye **gor**kee

тир

teer

электромобили

elektra-ma**bee**lee

сахарная вата

saharnaya **va**ta

Цирк tseerk

канатоходец
kanata-**ho**dyets

шест
shest

трапеция
tra**pyet**seeya

канат
ka**nat**

эквилибрист
ekvee-lee**breest**

верёвочная
лестница
vye**ryo**-vachnaya
lestneetsa

батут
ba**toot**

кролик
kroleek

акробаты
akra**ba**ti

дрессировщик
dryessee-**rov**shcheek

собака
sa**ba**ka

кольцо
kal'**tso**

цилиндр
tsee**leen**dr

жонглёр
zhan**glyor**

бабочка
babachka

оркестр
ar**kyes**tr

наездница
na**yez**neetsa

клоун
klo-oon

55

Word list

Here are all the Russian words in the book, in Cyrillic alphabetical order. To help you find words in the list, the Cyrillic alphabet is given below. Next to each word you can see how to pronounce it, in letters *like this*, and then its meaning in English.

а б в г д е ё ж з и й к л м н о п р с т у ф х ц ч ш щ ъ ы ь э ю я

а

абрикос, 34	abree**kos**	apricot
аварийная машина, 21	ava**ree**naya ma**shee**na	tow truck
автобус, 12	av**to**boos	bus
автомойка, 21	afta**moy**ka	car wash
автофургон, 23	aftafoor**gon**	camper
айсберг, 18	**ays**byerg	iceberg
аквариум, 29	ak**va**reeoom	aquarium
аккумулятор, 20	akoomoo-**lya**tar	battery
акробаты, 55	akra**ba**ti	acrobats
актёр, 40	ak**tyor**	actor
актриса, 40	ak**tree**sa	actress
акула, 19	a**koo**la	shark
алфавит, 29	alfa**veet**	alphabet
альпинизм, 51	al'pee**neezm**	climbing
амбар, 24	am**bar**	barn
американские горки, 54	ameree-**kan**skeeye **gor**kee	roller coaster, slide
американский футбол, 50	ameree**kan**skee foot**bol**	football
ананас, 35	ana**nas**	pineapple
антенна, 12	an**ten**na	antenna
антонимы, 44	an**to**neemi	opposites
апельсин, 31	apel'**seen**	orange (fruit)
аэропорт, 21	a-era**port**	airport

б

бабочка, 22	**ba**bachka	butterfly
бабочка, 55	**ba**bachka	bow tie
бабушка, 41	**ba**booshka	grandmother
багажник, 21	ba**gazh**neek	(car) trunk
бадминтон, 51	badmeen**ton**	badminton
байдарка, 27	bay**dar**ka	kayak
банан, 31	ba**nan**	banana
банка с краской, 11	**ban**ka s**kras**koy	paint can
банки, 11, 35	**ban**kee	jars
барабаны, 14	bara**ba**ni	drums
баржа, 23	**bar**zha	barge
барсук, 22	bar**sook**	badger
баскетбол, 50	baskyet**bol**	basketball
бассейн, 50	bas**seyn**	swimming pool
батарея, 5	bata**ryey**a	radiator
батут, 55	ba**toot**	safety net
бег, 50	**byeg**	race
бег трусцой, 51	**byeg** troos**tsoy**	jogging
бегемот, 18	bege**mot**	hippopotamus
бежать, 43	bye**zhat'**	to run
бейсбол, 50	beys**bol**	baseball
белка, 22	**byel**ka	squirrel
белый, 52	**byel**iy	white
белый медведь, 19	**byel**iy myed**vyed'**	polar bear
бензин, 21	byen**zeen**	gas
бензовоз, 21	byenza**voz**	tanker
бензоколонка, 21	byenzaka**lon**ka	gas pump
бечёвка, 17	bye**chov**ka	string
бизон, 19	bee**zon**	bison
бинт, 30	**beent**	bandage
бита, 50	**bee**ta	bat (sports)
близко, 44	**bleez**ka	near
блины, 36	blee**ni**	pancakes

блок-флейта, 14	blok-**flay**ta	recorder
блюдца, 7	**blyoot**sa	saucers
бобр, 19	**bo**br	beaver
бобы, 35	ba**bi**	beans
божья коровка, 8	**bozh'**ya ka**rov**ka	ladybug
больница, 30	bal'**neet**sa	hospital
большой, 44	bal'**shoy**	big
большой палец, 38	bal'**shoy** pa**lyets**	thumb
борьба сумо, 51	bar'**ba soo**mo	sumo wrestling
ботинки, 39	ba**teen**kee	shoes
бочка, 11	**boch**ka	barrel
брат, 41	**brat**	brother
брать, 43	**brat'**	to take
брёвна, 23	**bryov**na	logs
брикеты соломы, 25	bree**kye**ti sa**lo**mi	straw bales
бровь, 38	**brov'**	eyebrow
бросать, 42	bra**sat'**	to throw
брюки, 39	**bryoo**kee	pants
будка, 49	**boot**ka	kennel
булочки, 36	**boo**lachkee	bread rolls
бумага, 29	boo**ma**ga	paper
бусы, 14	**boo**si	beads
бутерброд, 33	bootyer**brod**	sandwich
бутылки, 35	boo**til**kee	bottles
буфера, 20	boo**fyer**a	buffers
бык, 24	**bik**	bull
быстро, 45	**bis**tra	fast

в

в школе, 28	v**shkol**ye	at school
вагоны, 20	va**go**ni	railway cars
ванна, 4	**van**na	bath
ванная, 4	**van**naya	bathroom
варёное яйцо, 36	va**ryon**aye yay**tso**	boiled egg
вата, 30	**va**ta	cotton balls
ведро, 26	vye**dro**	bucket
велосипед, 13	velasee**pyed**	bicycle
велоспорт, 51	vyela**sport**	cycling
верблюд, 19	vyer**blyood**	camel
верёвочная лестница, 55	vye**ryo**-vachnaya **lest**neetsa	rope ladder
верстак, 11	vyer**stak**	workbench
вертолёт, 20	vyerta**lyot**	helicopter
верхний, 44	**vyerh**nee	top
верховая езда, 51	vyerha**va**ya yez**da**	riding
весло, 26	vyes**lo**	oar
весло, 27	vyes**lo**	paddle
весна, 48	vyes**na**	spring
весы, 35	vye**si**	scales
ветврач, 49	vyet**vrach**	vet
ветер, 48	**vyet**yer	wind
ветки, 9	**vyet**kee	sticks
ветряная мельница, 22	vyetrya-**na**ya **myel'**neetsa	windmill
ветчина, 37	vyetchee**na**	ham
вечер, 46	**vyech**er	evening
вечеринка, 32	vyechee**reen**ka	party
вешалка, 5	**vye**shalka	coat rack
вёсельная лодка, 27	**vyo**sel'naya **lod**ka	rowboat
взлётная полоса, 21	vz**lyot**naya pala**sa**	runway
видеокассета, 5	veedeokas**syet**a	video

Ж

жаба, 23	*zha*ba	toad
жалюзи, 29	*zhal*yoozee	(window) blind
ждать, 43	*zhdat'*	to wait
железная дорога, 14	zhe*lyez*naya da*ro*ga	train set
железная дорога, 20	zhe*lyez*naya da*ro*ga	train track
жена, 41	zhe*na*	wife
жених, 47	zhe*neeh*	bridegroom
женщина, 13	*zhen*shcheena	woman
женщина-милиционер, 40	*zhen*shcheena-meelee-tseea*nyer*	policewoman
жёлтый, 52	*zhol*tiy	yellow
живая изгородь, 9	zhi*va*ya *eez*garad'	hedge
живой, 45	zhi*voy*	alive
живот, 38	zhi*vot*	tummy
жираф, 18	zhi*raf*	giraffe
жонглёр, 55	zhan*glyor*	juggler

З

забор, 17, 25	za*bor*	fence
завтрак, 36	*zav*trak	breakfast
закрытый, 44	za*kri*tiy	closed
залезать, 43	zalye*zat'*	to climb
замок, 14	*za*mak	castle
замок из песка, 26	*za*mak eez pyes*ka*	sandcastle
занавеска, 30	zana-*vyes*ka	curtain
занятия, 42	za*nya*teeya	doing things
звезда, 46, 52	zvyez*da*	star
зебра, 19	*zyeb*ra	zebra
зелёный, 52	zye*lyo*niy	green
земля, 17	zyem*lya*	dirt
земля, 24	zyem*lya*	mud
зеркало, 5	*zyer*kala	mirror
зима, 48	zee*ma*	winter
змея, 19	zme*ya*	snake
значок, 29	zna*chok*	badge
золотая рыбка, 49	zala*ta*ya *rib*ka	goldfish
зонтик, 26, 48	*zon*teek	umbrella
зоопарк, 18	zaa*park*	zoo
зубная паста, 4	zoob*na*ya *pas*ta	toothpaste
зубная щётка, 4	zoob*na*ya *shchot*ka	toothbrush
зубной врач, 41	zoob*noy vrach*	dentist
зубы, 38	*zoo*bi	teeth

И

игральные кости, 14	ee*gral'*niye *kos*tee	dice
играть, 43	ee*grat'*	to play
игрушки, 31, 32	ee*groosh*kee	toys
идти, 43	eed*tee*	to walk
индюки, 25	eendyoo*kee*	turkeys

Й

йогурт, 35	*yo*goort	yogurt

К

какао, 36	ka*ka*o	hot chocolate
календарь, 10, 46	kalyen*dar'*	calendar
калитка, 16	ka*leet*ka	gate
камни, 22	*kam*nee	stones
камни, 23	*kam*nee	rocks
канал, 23	ka*nal*	canal
канарейка, 49	kana*ryey*ka	canary
канат, 27	ka*nat*	rope
канат, 55	ka*nat*	tightrope
канатоходец, 55	kanata-*ho*dyets	tightrope walker
капот, 21	ka*pot*	(car) hood
капуста, 34	ka*poos*ta	cabbage
карандаш, 28	karan*dash*	pencil
карандаши, 29	karanda*shee*	crayons
каратэ, 50	kara*te*	karate
карманы, 39	*kar*mani	pockets
карта, 29	*kar*ta	map
картинка-конструктор, 30	kar*teen*ka-kan*strook*tar	jigsaw puzzle
картины, 5	kar*teen*i	pictures
картофель, 35, 37	kar*to*fel'	potatoes
картофельное пюре, 37	kar*to*fel'naye pyoo*re*	mashed potatoes
карусель, 54	karoo*syel'*	merry-go-round
касса, 35	*kas*sa	checkout
касса-автомат, 20	*kas*sa-avta*mat*	ticket machine
кассета, 33	kas*sye*ta	cassette tape
кастрюли, 6	kas*tryoo*lee	saucepans
каток, 13, 15	ka*tok*	steamroller
кафе, 12	ka-*fe*	cafe
кафель, 7	*ka*fyel'	tiles
качели, 16	ka*chye*lee	swings
качели, 17	ka*chye*lee	seesaw
квадрат, 52	kva*drat*	square
кенгуру, 18	kengoo*roo*	kangaroo
кепка, 39	*kyep*ka	cap
кинотеатр, 13	keena*teatr*	movie theater
кирпичи, 8	keerpee*chee*	bricks
кисточка, 29	*kees*toshka	(paint) brush
кисть руки, 38	*keest'* roo*kee*	hand
кит, 19	*keet*	whale
кладовка, 7	kla*dov*ka	(kitchen) closet
клей, 28	*kley*	glue
клетка, 49	*klyet*ka	cage
клоун, 55	*klo*-oon	clown
клубника, 33	kloob*nee*ka	strawberry
клумба, 17	*kloom*ba	flower bed
клюв, 49	*klyoof*	beak
ключ, 6	*klyooch*	key
книги, 28	*knee*gee	books
кнопки, 11	*knop*kee	tacks
кнопки, 28	*knop*kee	thumbtacks
ковёр, 4	ka*vyor*	carpet
коврик, 5	*kov*reek	rug
коза, 19	ka*za*	goat
колготки, 39	kal*got*kee	tights
колено, 38	ka*lye*na	knee
колесо, 20	ka*lye*so	wheel
колесо обозрения, 54	ka*lye*so aba-*zryen*eeya	Ferris wheel
колли, 24	*kol*lee	sheepdog
кольцо, 14	kal*'tso*	ring
кольцо, 55	kal*'tso*	hoop
коляска, 9	ka*lyas*ka	baby buggy
комиксы, 31	*ko*meeksi	comic
комод, 5	ka*mod*	chest of drawers
компакт-диск, 4	kam*pakt deesk*	CD
компьютер, 31	kamp'*yoo*ter	computer
консервы, 35	kan*syer*vi	cans
контролёр, 20	kantra*lyor*	conductor
конус, 52	*ko*noos	cone
конфета, 32	kan*fye*ta	candy
коньки, 51	kan'*kee*	ice skates
конюшня, 25	ka*nyoosh*nya	stable
копать, 42	ka*pat'*	to dig
копилка, 15	ka*peel*ka	(toy) bank
корабль, 27	ka*rabl'*	ship
корзина, 31, 35, 49	kar*zee*na	basket
коричневый, 52	ka*reech*nyeviy	brown
корм, 49	*korm*	pet food
коробка, 29	ka*rop*ka	box
корова, 25	ka*ro*va	cow
коровник, 25	ka*rov*neek	cowshed
короткий, 45	ka*rot*kee	short
космонавт, 40	kasma*naft*	astronaut
космонавты, 15	kasma*naf*ti	spacemen
космос, 46	*kos*mas	space
костёр, 9	kas*tyor*	bonfire
костыли, 30	kasti*lee*	crutches
кость, 9	*kost'*	bone
котёнок, 49	ka*tyo*nak	kitten

кофе, 36	**ko**fye	coffee
кофта, 39	**kof**ta	cardigan
кошелёк, 35	kashe**lyok**	coin purse
кошка, 49	**kosh**ka	cat
краб, 26	**krab**	crab
кран, 4	**kran**	faucet
краски, 15, 28	**kras**kee	paints
красный, 52	**kras**niy	red
кресло-каталка, 30	**kryes**la-ka**tal**ka	wheelchair
крикет, 50	**kree**kyet	cricket
кровать, 4	kra**vat'**	bed
крокодил, 18	kraka**deel**	crocodile
кролик, 49, 55	**kro**leek	rabbit
кроссовки, 39	kras**sov**kee	tennis shoes
крот, 23	**krot**	mole
круг, 52	**kroog**	circle
крыло, 18	kri**lo**	wing
крыша, 12	**kri**sha	roof
куб, 52	**koob**	cube
кубики, 14	**koo**beekee	blocks
куклы, 14	**kook**li	dolls
кукольный дом, 14	**koo**kal'niy **dom**	doll's house
купальник, 27	koo**pal'**neek	swimsuit
куртка, 39	**koort**ka	jacket
куры, 25	**koo**ri	hens
курятник, 24	koo**ryat**neek	hen house
куст, 16	**koost**	bush
кухня, 6	**kooh**nya	kitchen
кухонное полотенце, 7	**koo**hannaye pala**tyen**tse	dish towel

Л

лампа, 5	**lam**pa	lamp
лампочка, 33	**lam**pachka	light bulb
лапы, 18	**la**pi	paws
ласты, 27	**las**ti	flippers
лебеди, 17	**lye**bedee	swans
лев, 18	**lyev**	lion
левый, 44	**lyev**iy	left
легко, 45	lyeh**ko**	easy
лейка, 8	**ley**ka	watering can
лекарство, 30	lye**kar**stva	medicine
лента, 32	**lyen**ta	ribbon
леопард, 19	lyea**pard**	leopard
лес, 22	**lyes**	forest
лестница, 5	**lest**neetsa	stairs
лестница, 9, 10	**lest**neetsa	ladder
лестница, 13	**lest**neetsa	steps
лето, 48	**lye**ta	summer
летучая мышь, 18	lye**too**chaya **mish'**	bat (animal)
лимон, 34	lee**mon**	lemon
линейка, 28	lee**nyey**ka	ruler
лиса, 22	lee**sa**	fox
листья, 9	**leest'**ya	leaves
лисята, 23	lee**sya**ta	fox cubs
лифт, 30	**leeft**	elevator
лицо, 38	lee**tso**	face
ловить, 42	la**veet'**	to catch
ложки, 7	**lozh**kee	spoons
локомотив, 20	lakama**teev**	(train) engine
локоть, 38	**lo**kat'	elbow
ломать, 42	la**mat'**	to break
лопата, 8, 26	la**pa**ta	shovel
лошадь, 25, 51	**lo**shad'	horse
лошадь-качалка, 15	**lo**shad'-ka**chal**ka	rocking horse
лужа, 17	**loo**zha	puddle
лук, 15	**look**	bow
лук, 34	**look**	onion
лук-порей, 34	**look**-pa**rey**	leek
луна, 46	**loo**na	moon
луна-парк, 54	**loo**na-**park**	amusement park
лыжи, 51	**li**zhee	ski
лыжная палка, 51	**li**zhnaya **pal**ka	ski pole
львята, 18	l'**vya**ta	lion cubs

люди, 40	**lyoo**dee	people
лягушка, 16	lya**goosh**ka	frog

M

магазин, 12, 34	maga**zeen**	store
магазин игрушек, 14	maga**zeen** ee**groo**shek	toyshop
майка, 39	**may**ka	undershirt
маленький, 44	**ma**lyen'kee	small
малина, 33	ma**lee**na	raspberry
мало, 44	**ma**la	few
малыш, 17	ma**lish**	baby
мальчик, 28	**mal'**cheek	boy
маляр, 41	ma**lyar**	painter
мандарин, 33	manda**reen**	tangerine
марионетки, 15	mareea-**nyet**kee	puppets
маскарадные костюмы, 33	maska-**rad**niye kas**tyoo**mi	costumes
маски, 15	**mas**kee	masks
масло, 21	**mas**la	oil
масло, 33	**mas**la	butter
мастерская, 10	mastyer**ska**ya	workshop
мат, 54	**mat**	mat
мать, 41	**mat'**	mother
машина, 13	ma**shee**na	car
машинист, 20	mashee**neest**	engineer
маяк, 26	ma**yak**	lighthouse
медбрат, 30	myed**brat**	(male) nurse
медведь, 18	myed**vyed'**	bear
медленно, 45	**myed**lyenna	slow
мел, 28	**myel**	chalk
механики, 40	mye**ha**neekee	mechanics
мёд, 36	**myod**	honey
мёртвый, 45	**myort**viy	dead
милицейская машина, 12	meelee-**tsey**skaya ma**shee**na	police car
милиционер, 13, 40	meelee-tsee**a**nyer	policeman
миски, 7	**mees**kee	bowls
мишень, 51	mee**shyen'**	target
много, 44	**mno**ga	many
мойка, 6	**moy**ka	(kitchen) sink
мокрый, 44	**mok**riy	wet
молния, 39	**mol**neeya	zipper
молния, 48	**mol**neeya	lightning
молоко, 36, 49	mala**ko**	milk
молоток, 11	mala**tok**	hammer
мольберт, 29	mal'**byert**	easel
море, 26	**mo**rye	sea
морковь, 34	mar**kov'**	carrot
мороженое, 16	ma**ro**zhenaye	ice cream
мороз, 48	ma**roz**	frost
морская звезда, 26	mar**ska**ya zvyez**da**	starfish
морская свинка, 49	mar**ska**ya **sveen**ka	guinea pig
моряк, 26	ma**ryak**	sailor
мост, 23	**most**	bridge
моторка, 26	ma**tor**ka	motorboat
мотоцикл, 13	mata**tseek**l	motorcycle
мотыга, 8	ma**tee**ga	hoe
мотылёк, 23	matee**lyok**	moth
моя, 39	**ma**ya	my
муж, 41	**moozh**	husband
мужчина, 12	moozh**chee**na	man
мука, 35	moo**ka**	flour
мусор, 6	**moo**sar	trash
мусорное ведро, 29	**moo**sarnaye vye**dro**	wastepaper basket
мусорный бак, 8	**moo**sarniy **bak**	trash can
муха, 11	**moo**ha	fly
мыло, 4	**mi**la	soap
мыть, 42	**mit'**	to wash
мышь, 49	**mish'**	mouse
мягкий, 45	**myah**kee	soft
мясник, 40	myas**neek**	butcher
мясо, 35	**mya**sa	meat
мяч, 17, 50	**myach**	ball

60

покупать, 43	pakoo**pat'**	to buy
пол, 29	**pol**	floor
поле, 25	**pol**ye	field
ползти, 42	pal**stee**	to crawl
поливальная установка, 8	palee-**val'**naya oosta**nov**ka	sprinkler
полный, 45	**pol**niy	full
полотенце, 4	pala**tyen**tse	towel
полумесяц, 52	paloo-**myes**yats	crescent
помидор, 34	pamee**dor**	tomato
понедельник, 46	panye**dyel'**neek	Monday
пони, 51	**po**nee	pony
попкорн, 54	pap**korn**	popcorn
попугай, 49	papoo**gay**	parrot
поросята, 25	para**sya**ta	piglets
последний, 44	pa**slyed**nee	last
потолок, 29	pata**lok**	ceiling
почтальон, 41	pachtal'**on**	mail carrier
правый, 45	**pra**viy	right
праздники, 47	**praz**neekee	special days
праздничный торт, 47	**praz**neechniy **tort**	birthday cake
приёмная, 31	pree**yom**naya	waiting room
примеры, 28	pree**myer**i	math problems
прицеп, 13	pree**tsep**	trailer
прогулочная коляска, 17	pra**goo**-lachnaya ka**lyas**ka	stroller
простыня, 5	prasti**nya**	sheet
пруд, 24	**prood**	pond
прыгать, 42	**pri**gat'	to skip
прыгать, 43	**pri**gat'	to jump
прыжки в воду, 50	prish**kee vvo**doo	diving
пряжка, 39	**pryash**ka	buckle
прямоугольник, 52	pryama-oo**gol'**neek	rectangle
прятаться, 43	**prya**tat'sa	to hide
птицы, 17	**ptee**tsi	birds
пугало, 25	**poo**gala	scarecrow
пуговицы, 39	**poo**gaveetsi	buttons
пудинг, 37	**poo**deeng	dessert
пурпурный, 52	poor**poor**niy	purple
пустой, 45	poo**stoy**	empty
путешествие, 20	pootye-**shest**veeye	travel
пуховое одеяло, 5	poo**ho**vaye adye**ya**la	comforter
пчела, 9	pchye**la**	bee
пылесос, 6	pilye**sos**	vacuum cleaner
пятнадцать, 53	pyat**nat**sat'	fifteen
пятница, 46	**pyat**neetsa	Friday
пять, 53	**pyat'**	five

р

радио, 4	**ra**deeo	radio
радуга, 48	**ra**dooga	rainbow
разговаривать, 42	razga-**va**reevat'	to talk
раздевалка, 51	razdye-**val**ka	changing room
ракета, 15	ra**kyet**a	rocket
ракета, 46	ra**kyet**a	spaceship
ракетка, 50	ra**kyet**ka	racket
раковина, 4	**ra**kaveena	(bathroom) sink
раковина, 26	**ra**kaveena	shell
растение, 29	ra**styen**eeye	plant
расчёска, 5	ras**chos**ka	comb
регби, 50	**reg**bee	rugby
резать, 42	**ryez**at'	to cut
резинка, 28	rye**zeen**ka	eraser
река, 22	rye**ka**	river
ремень, 39	rye**men'**	belt
рис, 37	**rees**	rice
рисовать, 42	reesa**vat'**	to paint
рисунок, 28	ree**soo**nak	drawing
робот, 14	**ro**bat	robot
рога, 19	ra**ga**	horns
Рождество, 47	razhdest**vo**	Christmas day
розовый, 52	**ro**zaviy	pink
ролики, 16	**ro**leekee	roller blades
ромб, 52	**romb**	diamond

роса, 48	ra**sa**	dew
рот, 38	**rot**	mouth
рояль, 15	ra**yal'**	piano
рубанок, 11	roo**ban**ak	shaving plane
рубашка, 39	roo**bash**ka	shirt
рубить, 42	roo**beet'**	to chop
ружьё, 15	roozh'**yo**	gun
рука, 38	roo**ka**	arm
рулетка, 11	roo**lyet**ka	tape measure
ручей, 22	roo**chey**	stream
ручка, 28	**rooch**ka	pen
рыба, 27	**ri**ba	fish
рыбак, 23	ri**bak**	fisherman
рыбалка, 50	ri**bal**ka	fishing
рыбачья лодка, 27	ri**bach'**ya **lod**ka	fishing boat
рынок, 13	**ri**nak	market
рюкзак, 20	ryook**zak**	backpack

с

сад, 8	**sad**	yard
сад, 25	**sad**	orchard
салат, 34	sa**lat**	lettuce
салат, 37	sa**lat**	salad
салфетки, 31	sal**fyet**kee	tissues
салями, 33	sa**lya**mee	salami
самолёт, 21	sama**lyot**	plane
сандали, 39	san**da**lee	sandals
сани, 47	**sa**nee	sleigh
сапоги, 39	sapa**gee**	boots
сарай, 8	sa**ray**	shed
сахар, 36	**sa**har	sugar
сахарная вата, 54	**sa**harnaya **va**ta	cotton candy
свадьба, 47	**svad'**ba	wedding day
светло, 45	svyet**lo**	light
светофор, 13	svyeta**for**	traffic lights
свеча, 32, 47	svye**cha**	candle
свинарник, 24	svee**nar**neek	pigsty
свиньи, 25	**sveen'**ee	pigs
свисток, 14	svee**stok**	whistle
свитер, 39	**svee**ter	sweatshirt
северный олень, 47	**syev**erniy a**len'**	reindeer
седло, 25	syed**lo**	saddle
сельдерей, 34	syel'**de**rey	celery
сельская местность, 22	**syel'**skaya **myest**nast'	country
семафор, 20	sema**for**	signals
семена, 8	syeme**na**	seeds
семнадцать, 53	syem**nat**sat'	seventeen
семь, 53	**syem'**	seven
семья, 41	syem'**ya**	families
сено, 25	**sye**na	hay
серый, 52	**syer**iy	gray
сестра, 41	sye**stra**	sister
сеть, 27	**syet'**	net
сзади, 45	s**za**dee	behind
сидеть, 43	see**dyet'**	to sit
синий, 52	**see**nee	blue
скакалка, 17	ska**kal**ka	jump rope
скамейка, 16	ska**myey**ka	bench
скатерть, 33	**ska**tyert'	tablecloth
скейтборд, 17	skeyt**bord**	skateboard
сковорода, 7	skavara**da**	frying pan
скорая помощь, 12	**sko**raya **po**mashch'	ambulance
слива, 35	**slee**va	plum
сливки, 36	**sleev**kee	cream
слон, 19	**slon**	elephant
слушать, 42	**sloo**shat'	to listen
смеяться, 42	sme**yat'**sa	to laugh
смотреть, 43	sma**tryet'**	to watch
снаружи, 45	sna**roo**zhee	out
снег, 48	**snyeg**	snow
сноубординг, 50	sno-oo**bor**deeng	snowboarding
собака, 16, 49, 55	sa**ba**ka	dog
собирать, 43	sabee**rat'**	to pick

сова, 23	*sava*	owl
совок, 7	*savok*	dustpan
совок, 9	*savok*	trowel
солдатики, 15	*saldateekee*	soldiers
солнце, 46, 48	*solntse*	sun
соломинка, 32	*salomeenka*	straw
соль, 36	*sol'*	salt
сосиска, 33	*saseeska*	sausage
соус, 37	*so-oos*	ketchup
софа, 4	*safa*	sofa
спагетти, 37	*spagettee*	spaghetti
спальня, 5	*spal'nya*	bedroom
спать, 43	*spat'*	to sleep
спереди, 45	*speryedee*	in front
спина, 38	*speena*	back (of body)
спички, 7	*speechkee*	matches
спорт, 50	*sport*	sport
среда, 46	*sryeda*	Wednesday
стаканы, 6	*stakani*	glasses (for drinking)
старый, 45	*stariy*	old
стена, 29	*styena*	wall
стиральная машина, 7	*steeral'naya masheena*	washing mashine
стиральный порошок, 6	*steeral'niy parashok*	laundry detergent
стог, 24	*stok*	haystack
стол, 5	*stol*	table
страус, 18	*straoos*	ostrich
стрелы, 14	*stryeli*	arrows
стрельба из лука, 51	*stryel'ba eez looka*	archery
стружки, 10	*strooshkee*	shavings
стул, 5	*stool*	chair
ступня, 38	*stoopnya*	foot
стюард, 21	*styooard*	flight attendant (man)
стюардесса, 21	*styooardessa*	flight attendant (woman)
суббота, 46	*soobbota*	Saturday
судья, 40	*sood'ya*	judge
сумочка, 35	*soomachka*	purse
суп, 37	*soop*	soup
сухой, 44	*soohoy*	dry
сын, 41	*sin*	son
сыр, 33, 34	*seer*	cheese

T

таблетки, 30	*tablyetkee*	pills
табурет, 6	*tabooryet*	stool
такси, 13	*taksee*	taxi
танкер, 27	*tankyer*	oil tanker
танцевать, 42	*tantsevat'*	to dance
танцоры, 40	*tantsori*	dancers
танцы, 50	*tantsi*	dance
тарелки, 7	*taryelkee*	plates
тачка, 8	*tachka*	wheelbarrow
твёрдый, 45	*tvyordiy*	hard
телевизор, 31	*televeezar*	television
тележка, 24, 35	*tyelyeshka*	cart
телескоп, 46	*tyeleskop*	telescope
телефон, 5	*telefon*	telephone
телёнок, 25	*tyelyonak*	calf
темно, 45	*tyemno*	dark
теннис, 50	*tennees*	tennis
теплица, 9	*tyepleetsa*	greenhouse
термометр, 30	*tyermometr*	thermometer
тетрадь, 29	*tyetrad'*	notebook
тётя, 41	*tyotya*	aunt
тигр, 19	*teegr*	tiger
тир, 54	*teer*	rifle range
тиски, 10	*teeskee*	vise
товарный поезд, 20	*tavarniy poyest*	freight train
толкать, 43	*talkat'*	to push
толстый, 44	*tolstiy*	fat
тонкий, 44	*tonkee*	thin

топор, 11	*tapor*	ax
торт, 32	*tort*	cake
тосты, 36	*tosti*	toast
трава, 9	*trava*	grass
трактор, 24	*traktar*	tractor
трапеция, 55	*trapyetseeya*	trapeze
треугольник, 52	*trye-oogol'neek*	triangle
трёхколесный велосипед, 17	*tryohkal-yosniy vyela-seepyed*	tricycle
три, 53	*tree*	three
тринадцать, 53	*treenatsat'*	thirteen
тропинка, 9, 16	*trapeenka*	path
тротуар, 12	*tratooar*	pavement
труба, 12	*trooba*	chimney
труба, 14	*trooba*	trumpet
трубы, 12	*troobi*	pipes
трудно, 45	*troodna*	difficult
трусы, 39	*troosee*	underwear
тряпка для пыли, 7	*tryapka dlya pilee*	dust cloth
туалетная бумага, 4	*tooalyet-naya boomaga*	toilet paper
туман, 48	*tooman*	fog, mist
туннель, 23	*toonel'*	tunnel
тыква, 35	*tikva*	pumpkin
тюлень, 19	*tyoolen'*	seal
тянуть, 43	*tyanoot'*	to pull

У

у моря, 26	*oo morya*	seaside
удочка, 50	*oodachka*	fishing rod
ужин, 37	*oozheen*	dinner, supper
улей, 8	*ooley*	beehive
улитка, 8	*ooleetka*	snail
улица, 12	*ooleetsa*	street
уличный фонарь, 13	*ooleechniy fanar'*	lamp post
улыбаться, 42	*oolibat'sa*	to smile
унитаз, 4	*ooneetaz*	toilet
утёс, 27	*ootyos*	cliff
утки, 17, 24	*ootkee*	ducklings
утро, 46	*ootra*	morning
утюг, 7	*ootyoog*	iron
утята, 17, 24	*ootyata*	ducks
учительница, 29	*oocheetel'neetsa*	teacher
уши, 38	*ooshee*	ears

Ф

фабрика, 13	*fabreeka*	factory
фартук, 6	*fartook*	apron
фары, 20	*fari*	headlights
фейерверк, 32	*feyervyerk*	fireworks
ферма, 24	*fyerma*	farm
фермер, 25	*fyermyer*	farmer
фигурное катание, 51	*feegoornaye kataneeye*	ice-skating
фигуры, 52	*feegoori*	shapes
физкультура, 50	*feeskool'-toora*	exercise
флаг, 26	*flag*	flag
фломастеры, 28	*flamasteri*	felt-tip pens
фотоаппарат, 14, 47	*fota-apparat*	camera
фотограф, 47	*fatograf*	photographer
фотографии, 28	*fatagrafee*	photographs
фруктовый сок, 33	*frooktoviy sok*	fruit juice
фрукты, 34	*frookti*	fruit
фургон, 13	*foorgon*	van
футбол, 51	*footbol*	soccer
футболка, 39	*footbolka*	T-shirt

Х

халат, 30	*halat*	bathrobe
хвост, 18	*hvost*	tail
хлеб, 33	*hlyeb*	bread
хлопья, 36	*hlop'ya*	cereal

хобот, 19	**хо**bot	(elephant's) trunk
холл, 5	**holl**	hall
холм, 23	**holm**	hill
холодильник, 6	hala**deel'**neek	refrigerator
холодный, 44	ha**lod**niy	cold
хомяк, 49	ha**myak**	hamster
хороший, 44	ha**ro**shee	good
художник, 40	hoo**dozh**neek	artist

Ц

цвета, 52	tsvye**ta**	colors
цветная капуста, 34	tsvyet**naya ka**poosta	cauliflower
цветы, 8	tsvye**ti**	flowers
цилиндр, 55	tsee**leen**dr	top hat
цирк, 55	**tseerk**	circus
цистерна, 24	tsees**ter**na	tanker
цыплёнок, 37	tsi**plyo**nak	chicken
цыплята, 24	tsi**plya**ta	chicks

Ч

чай, 36	**chay**	tea
чайка, 26	**chay**ka	sea gull
чайник, 7	**chay**neek	kettle
чайник, 36	**chay**neek	teapot
чайные ложки, 6	**chay**niye **lozh**kee	teaspoons
часы, 6	cha**si**	clock
часы, 30	cha**si**	watch
чашки, 7	**chash**kee	cups
чемодан, 20	chema**dan**	suitcase
червяк, 8	cher**vyak**	worm
чердак, 24	cher**dak**	hayloft
черепаха, 19	chere**pa**ha	tortoise
четверг, 46	chet**vyerg**	Thursday
четыре, 53	che**tir**ye	four
четырнадцать, 53	che**tir**-natsat'	fourteen
чёрный, 52	**chor**niy	black
чипсы, 33	**cheep**si	chips
чипсы, 37	**cheep**si	French fries
числа, 53	**chees**la	numbers
чистый, 44	**chees**tiy	clean
читать, 43	chee**tat'**	to read

Ш

шарики, 15	**sha**reekee	marbles
шарф, 39	**sharf**	scarf
швабра, 7	**shva**bra	mop
шезлонг, 27	shez**long**	beach chair
шест, 55	**shest**	pole
шестнадцать, 53	shest**nat**sat'	sixteen

шесть, 53	**shest'**	six
шея, 38	**she**ya	neck
шина, 21	**shee**na	tire
шить, 43	**sheet'**	to sew
шкаф, 5	**shkaf**	(bedroom) closet
шкафчик, 51	**shkaf**cheek	locker
школа, 12	**shko**la	school
шланг, 9	**shlang**	garden hose
шлем, 51	**shlyem**	helmet
шлёпанцы, 31	**shlyo**pantsi	slippers
шлюз, 22	**shlyooz**	lock
шляпа, 27	**shlya**pa	sunhat
шляпа, 39	**shlya**pa	hat
шнурок, 39	shnoo**rok**	shoelace
шоколад, 32	shaka**lad**	chocolate
шорты, 39	**shor**ti	shorts
шпинат, 35	shpee**nat**	spinach
шприц, 30	**shpreets**	syringe
шурупы, 10	shoo**roo**pi	screws

Щ

щека, 38	shche**ka**	cheek
щенок, 49	shche**nok**	puppy
щётка, 5, 7	**shchot**ka	brush
щётка, 7	**shchot**ka	broom

Э

эквилибрист, 55	ekvee-lee**breest**	unicyclist
экскаватор, 12	ekska**va**tar	bulldozer
электромобили, 54	elektra-ma**bee**lee	bumper cars

Ю

юбка, 39	**yoop**ka	skirt

Я

я, 38	**ya**	me
яблоко, 30	**ya**blaka	apple
ягнята, 24	yag**nya**ta	lambs
ягодицы, 38	yaga**dee**tsi	bottom (of body)
язык, 38	ya**zik**	tongue
яичница, 36	ya**eech**neetsa	fried egg
яйца, 35	**yay**tsa	eggs
яма, 12	**ya**ma	hole
яхта, 15, 17	**yah**ta	toy boat
ящерица, 22	**yash**chereetsa	lizard
ящик, 7	**yash**cheek	drawer
ящик для инструментов, 10	**yash**cheek dlya eenstroo-**myen**tav	tool box

Designed by Andy Griffin
Cover design by Hannah Ahmed

This revised edition first published in 2005 by Usborne Publishing Ltd., Usborne House, 83-85 Saffron Hill, London EC1N 8RT, England. www.usborne.com